My Childhood Inspirations The Series
Book 2:
Little Girl
Remembers

by

Joyce Green

Copyright © 2017 by Joyce Green

All rights reserved. This book or any portion thereof may not be reproduced or used in any manner whatsoever without the express written permission of the author and/or publisher except for the use of brief quotations in a book review. The Old MacDonald lyrics used in this book are in the public domain.

Illustrator: Jucalstudios@gmail.com

Publisher: G Publishing LLC

ISBN: 978-0-9969684-1-6

Library of Congress Control Number: 2015920431

Published and Printed in the United States of America

Warm Acknowledgements to my Grandchildren
for Ideas and Insights!

Shaydon Simpson

Sheyenne Simpson

Sequoyeth Simpson

I wrote these true stories for my grandchildren.

Barbara and Iris

I'm an Airplane Pilot

What Happened to the Cat

"My Hero"

Singing the Lord's Prayer in Church

Barbara and Iris

I grew up in a small suburban New York town called Hempstead. My family moved to Hempstead in the 1940s before I was born. At that time, the majority of Hempstead's population was White. The Colored people (as we were called then) made up about 5 - 10 percent of the population.

Our neighborhood was all White when my family moved there. Our house had been previously owned by a fireman and his family.

There were three empty lots and two big fields near our house. My brothers used to play baseball in the lot across the street from our house. They had to stop playing there, though, because they kept hitting balls that broke the neighbor's windows.

There were lots of apple trees and blackberry bushes where we lived. At the end of the summer, we had to pick blackberries and Ma would make blackberry dumplings and blackberry cobbler……*Ooo*, it was *sooooo* good.

We had a pear tree and four apple trees in our yard. There was a mulberry tree on the side of our house next to a chestnut tree. In our backyard was a wild grapevine. In our front yard, we had three big honeysuckle bushes, some hedges, and two tall oak trees. Elm and hickory trees dotted the neighborhood. There was a little crab-apple orchard on the left side of the street a half-block away from our house.

Ma grew some beautiful flowers next to an apple tree on the side of our driveway. Ma had planted red and off-white roses in the backyard. She had daffodils, white coral shells, pansies, and yellow tulips there too. The flowers were beautiful.

One of those three empty lots in the neighborhood was right next to our house. Ma would plant vegetables in that big lot. She had tomatoes, carrots, stringbeans, and other crops in that garden. Ma was raised on a farm in North Carolina; she knew how to grow a lot of things.

I had two friends who lived three blocks from my house. Barbara, who was White, and Iris, who was Jewish. I met Barbara and Iris when we were in kindergarten.

I used to go to Barbara's house to play when Mommy went shopping at the corner meat market and grocery stores. Those stores were a half-block up the street from Barbara and Iris' house.

Barbara's mommy called Barbara "Barbie," so I did, too. Barbie was little, pudgy, and cute. She had brown curly hair all over her head.

When I was visiting Barbie, she and I would play in the grass on the side of her house. Mommy would come and get me after she had finished shopping and it was time to go home.

One early afternoon, Mommy dropped me off at Barbie's house while she went to the corner supermarket. Mommy was at the store for only a little while. Then she came back to get me. We were going home.

This day, Barbie wanted me to stay over her house and play with her. She was an only child and liked my company. But Mommy had too much to do at home to leave me there and then come back for me. When Mommy came to get me, I was sad too. I liked playing with Barbie.

"I want her to stay here with me," screamed Barbie to her Mommy. My Mommy looked at Barbie's Mommy and then said to Barbie, "Joyce has to go home today because I got a lot of work to do. I won't have time to come back to get her."

"I want her to stay here," said Barbie.

"But she has to go home with her Mommy," said Barbie's Mommy.

Barbie started screaming, "*No! NO!*"

By now, Barbie was throwing a tantrum. She threw herself on the ground and began screaming and kicking her feet in the air. Her face was turning red, and tears were running down her cheeks.

Barbie's Mommy didn't know what to do. Barbie was out of control. I looked at Mommy, puzzled. I never saw Barbie act like this before.

Then Barbie announced, "I'm going to her house to play."

Mommy was quiet. So was I. Back then, White children never visited Colored children at Colored children's homes. But little Barbie hardly knew that; she wanted to play and was adamant.

Barbie's Mommy wrung her hands. She didn't know what to do. But, because Barbie's mommy and my mommy were real friendly, Mommy said, "You know what? Maybe you can come over to our house and play for a little while."

Barbie stood up. Her tear-stained face lit up with a big smile. "Yaaaay," she said.

My Mommy looked at Barbie's Mommy. "She can come over for about an hour now," said Mommy, "I'll take care of her; she'll be all right."

Barbie was all ready to go.

Reluctantly Barbie's Mommy let Barbie come over to our house.

When we got home, Barbie and I started playing in the front yard. Then my brothers came home from school for lunch.

My brothers were always laughing, yelling, and boxing each other when they came home.

When my brothers saw Barbie, they were surprised. They looked curiously at this little White girl in our front yard. Then they shrugged and continued doing what they were doing. But my brothers were so loud and noisy I think they scared Barbie a lot. She started crying uncontrollably. She wanted to go home.

"Mommy, Mommy, Barbie's crying again," I yelled.

Mommy came out of the house real fast. She grabbed Barbie's hand, and Barbie grabbed Mommy's leg.

"I want to go home" screamed Barbie.

"All right," said Mommy.

Holding Barbie's hand, Mommy walked her and me down the street to Barbie's house.

When we got to Barbie's house, Barbie ran to her back door, calling her Mommy.

After Mommy and I took Barbie home, we started walking back home. We turned the corner and walked in silence, passing the crabapple orchard.

I looked at the trees on both sides of the street. They were the same for everybody. I wondered, *Why did people have to act so different?*

That's the only time Barbie came over to my house. After that, Barbie and I only played together at school.

Iris, who was Jewish, lived across the street from Barbie. She had straight black hair to her shoulders. She had short bangs and wore glasses.

Iris was thin and taller than me. She was also real loud and a little bossy. She liked to tell everybody what to do, even her parents.

We became friends when we started walking home from school together. (Mommy would let me visit Iris, but I mostly saw her in school.)

When we were about nine years old, Iris had a birthday party and invited me. I went to Iris's house the day of the party. Everyone was in the backyard. They were mostly Jewish.

I stood in the driveway, at the front of their house, thinking, *Should I go back home or go in?*

Just then Iris' father saw me and called out to Iris, "Iris, your friend Joyce is here"

Iris came running out of the backyard, yelling my name, "Joyce, Joyce! Come in the back!" Her father began following her shortly after. "Come in, come in," yelled Iris' father.

As I walked down the driveway, Iris ran towards me. She looked very pretty. She had on a white dress that was very frilly and maybe black shoes. On top of her head was a pretty white satin bow.

Iris grabbed a scrawny thin-looking Jewish boy and was pulling him with her on the way to meet me.

"This is my boyfriend," she shouted, and then she grabbed him and kissed him—RIGHT ON THE MOUTH!—with her Daddy standing right there! But her Daddy just continued to stand there, grinning.

Well! ... I was shocked! My mouth fell open. I thought, *If my Daddy saw me kiss a boy, that might be the end of me.* I probably would have to run and hide to avoid a stinging whipping.

Iris' Daddy saw the confused look on my face. He laughed real hard and was really tickled by the expression on my face.

I had fun at Iris' party. We played games like Pin the Tail on the Donkey. When I went home, I told Mommy "Iris has a boyfriend and she kissed him on the mouth in front of her Daddy.". Mommy laughed and shook her head saying, "I know you know better!" "Yep," I said while thinking about what Daddy would do to me.

Even though Barbara lived across the street from Iris, she stayed away from Iris and her party. Barbara and Iris went their separate ways, and so did their parents. I always wondered why.

A year later Barbara and her family moved away. Three years later, Iris and her family moved. They were nice friends for a while.

I'm an Airplane Pilot

My brother Toojie was just like my Daddy. He loved mechanical things and things that fly.

One day, I saw Toojie pulling a raggedy baby carriage into our yard. "What are you doing," I asked?

" I'm gonna make an airplane," he said.

I couldn't believe it at first. "You are?" I asked.

"Yes," he said.

"How you gonna do that?" I asked.

"By building it," he said.

"Can I watch," I asked?

"You can watch," he allowed, "but don't get in my way."

"Okay," I agreed.

Toojie took the wheels off the baby carriage and laid them on the ground.

In those days, every neighborhood had a milkman. The milkman delivered bottles of milk in crates to your porch early in the morning. Sometimes, he would leave an empty crate on the porch. We had two old ones in our garage.

Toojie drug one crate out of the garage and put it next to the baby-carriage wheels, then went back into the garage, where Daddy kept his tools.

Daddy was a carpenter, and he had all sorts of carpenter stuff in the garage. Toojie took one of Daddy's little saws from one of Daddy's tool boxes.

Daddy taught all my brothers how to saw wood. Daddy showed them how to use a saw on a wooden sawing horse while cutting wood. Daddy taught me too.

Tooji cut out one side of the milk crate. The milk crate was going to be the seat of the airplane, he explained. Then Toojie went to the side of the garage where Daddy had a lot of wood planks and boards. He pulled out maybe three long planks and two boards.

Daddy always had nails in the garage, so Toojie helped himself.

Next, Toojie got a hammer.

My brother Toojie was really busy making this airplane. I watched him for a while. Then I got bored.

"Where you going?" shouted Toojie as he watched me run to the back door of our house.

"I'm tired, I'm going in the house," I said. Toojie said nothing. He just continued to build his airplane.

I went inside. I was sleepy. I took a nap.

Later that afternoon, after a good nap, I went back outside. I wanted to see if Toojie was still there. Yep, he was!

Toojie made a big long box, maybe five feet long, out of those wood planks and a board. He left one side of the box open. Then he put the milk crate in the open side of the box for a seat.

Toojie banged each carriage wheel to a plank. The planks were all different sizes, but each was real long, so Toojie cut them in half.

It looked real strange to me. I left to go to the half-a-house to play with my friend Gail.

A little later, I heard Ma calling me. I left Gail and ran home. I looked for my brother Toojie, but he was gone.

That evening, while sitting at the dinner table, I asked Toojie, "Where is the airplane?"

Toojie's eyes got real big. "What airplane?" he asked.

"The airplane you're making," I said.

Nobody batted an eyelash. I guess they thought Toojie was making a drawing—he was really good at drawing. Or maybe they thought he was making a little toy airplane.

"Shush, shush," he told me, real low. I was a little confused when he said "Shah" to me, trying to make me be quiet. Toojie looked at me and I looked at him.

Then, when Ma and my sister started talking, Toojie whispered to me, "It's a secret."

"Why?" I asked.

"It's a surprise," he said. "When I'm finished, you can help me test it out and show everybody, okay?"

"Okay," I whispered back. Then I started giggling. I had a secret.

A few minutes later, I forgot about the airplane and the secret. The next morning, after Daddy went to work, Toojie went to his secret hiding place behind the old garage and pulled out the box he'd made. The box still had the milk-crate seat in it, but it was all dirty and wet because it had rained overnight. That box was real "ucky."

"When I finish building this airplane, you can be the pilot," said Toojie.

"Nope," I said, I ain't sittin' in that wet dirty old box."

"This is not a *box!*" Toojie screamed at me. "It's the cockpit!"

"What's a cockpit?" I asked.

"It's the place where the pilot sits and steers the plane."

"Nope," I said again and ran to the back path to the half-a-house to play with my friend Gail.

It got real hot outside that day. Gail said, "It's hot. I'm going home."

"Okay, I'm going home too," I said. But, before I could, Toojie came to get me.

"What are you doin'?" he asked.

"I was playing with Gail," I said.

"Ma is looking for you. Come on" he said.

I followed him home.

When we came through the back path to the garage, I saw that Toojie had nailed the cut wooden planks with their attached carriage wheels to the box.

I just stood there and looked at it, and looked at it, and looked at it.... Finally, I asked, "What's *that*?"

"It's my airplane," he said.

"Don't look like a airplane to me. It looks like a broke toy turkey with no head," I said.

Toojie rolled his eyes at me with disgust and then he looked at the box on baby-carriage wheels. He was furious with me for insulting his masterpiece. I ran in the house.

Ma yelled at me when I came in the house. I had stayed at the half-a-house too long. I ate my peanut-butter-and-jelly sandwich and drank my milk. Then, because it was so hot, I lay down in the play room and fell asleep.

When I woke up, I heard Ma laughing real hard. She was in the backyard. *Uh-oh. I wonder if she saw Toojie's airplane.* I got up and ran outside.

Toojie had been busy. He had found a lawn mower on the street. The blades were all bent up in it, but the neighbor who threw it out told Toojie it still had a working motor and that Toojie could have the mower if he wanted.

So Toojie took the motor out of the lawn mower. Then he took the carriage wheel legs off the box. He pulled out a bigger wood plank from the shed. He nailed that plank to the bottom of the box. The plank was longer in the front than the back of the box. Toojie nailed another short piece of wood across the front of the long board that was nailed to the bottom of the box. Then he tied the motor on to the front of the box where the wood boards were nailed across each other.

Toojie nailed the carriage wheels back on the box. He tied a jump rope to the front wheels and pulled the rope to the front of the box.

Toojie made a propeller all by himself. Now that propeller looked like the real thing. It was long and curly. Toojie took a steering wheel from somebody's old car. He even found a long rubber hose in that old car too. He used that rubber hose in the airplane. He put the propeller in front of the airplane.

That's when Ma came outside. She caught Toojie off guard when she came outside unexpectedly. She saw Toojie's airplane and was stunned at the sight of it. Ma started laughing and laughing.

Well, Toojie thought Ma was laughing at him. She was … sort of. She was laughing in sheer amazement. Ma had to sit down on the back steps because she was so tickled. Ma just covered her mouth in amazement. Ma tried to talk to Toojie, but she was just overcome with amusement.

Ma's laughter just made Toojie angry. Every time Ma tried to say something, she would start laughing again. Ma was laughing so much that I started laughing with her.

Toojie got real upset. He slowly pulled the airplane to the side of the garage, and then one of the legs with the carriage wheel on it broke off. Toojie slammed the airplane on the garage wall and ran into the house.

I think Ma felt real bad about laughing at Toojie's airplane because, later that night, Ma told Toojie a story about Daddy trying to make our stove into a gas stove.

"… Then it blew up and caught on fire. Your Daddy fixed it and then went outside to make something else," Ma told Toojie ."You're just like your Daddy. He's always making things, and you make things real good too."

Maybe Toojie believed her. He wouldn't say anything, though.

The next day, guess who was outside fixing that broken airplane ... Toojie.

It rained that night, and it rained for the next three days. Toojie tried to work on his airplane in the garage, but it was too wet.

After the rain, the next few days were sticky and hot. Toojie worked on the airplane, and three days later he told me, "It's ready. Tomorrow morning you can be the pilot. I found a nice pillow to put in the cockpit You can sit on it and be the pilot. You're just the right size."

Right after Daddy left for work, Toojie said, "Let's go!" Toojie's airplane was real big now. From the side of the garage, he pulled the airplane down the driveway to the street. It was lopsided.

"Come on," he said.

"It's a little crooked," I said as I ran behind the airplane to the end of the driveway.

Toojie said, "See if anybody is lookin'."

I looked. It was about 8:30 in the morning. Everybody was still in their houses.

"Get in! I'll help you," said Toojie.

I got in.

The airplane was bigger than I thought. My head didn't come up to the steering wheel. "Okay, get ready," said Toojie.

"Okay," I said.

Toojie started winding up the propeller. "Hold the steering wheel tight and straight. Don't turn the wheel," he said.

"Okay," I said.

Then Toojie ran to the back of the airplane and began pushing it with all his might down the street. I couldn't see nothing.

Claxity claxity clax went the airplane. The wheels were bumping and rolling except for one on the left side. I slid to the lower side of the airplane.

Toojie was yelling, "Hold the steering wheel real tight."

Too late. The airplane was moving faster than Toojie could run behind it, and I was scared.

Then one of the carriage wheels broke, and the airplane looped about five feet off the ground, zoomed in the air and crashed into the lot half way down the street.

Toojie yelled in horror. He came running to the crash site. I had bumped my face against that steering wheel, and my mouth was bleeding. There was a little blood on my knee, too.

By now, I was crying. I had a big bruise on my forehead where I had bumped my head on the steering wheel, and a knot was coming out.. My arm and one leg were bruised and real sore.

"Are you all right," yelled Toojie as he came running up to the crash. He was real scared.

Toojie pulled the wood and motor away to get me out.

"Everything hurts." I yelled, crying real hard.

Toojie knew he was in BIG trouble.

"Come on, I'll take you home," he said.

"No," I said, "leave me alone!"

I slowly hobbled down the street home. I was real mad at Toojie.

When Ma saw me, her face squinted up. I started crying again.

"What happened to you?" she shouted.

"I was the pilot in Toojie's airplane, and it crashed into the field.

"WHAT!! *What airplane?*" she yelled.

"Toojie's airplane," I said tearfully.

Ma mumbled as she cleaned me up. Then she asked, "Where's your brother?"

"In the field down the street," I said.

Ma took off out the door. I knew Toojie was going to really get it. I hobbled upstairs to lie down in my room. I felt better in about three days.

Toojie was real quiet for the next few weeks. I never saw that airplane again. Especially after Daddy got home and found out what happened.

Little did I know that, years later, Toojie would make a one-man helicopter that would get almost 20 feet off the ground. Toojie was a great inventor!

What Happened to the Cat?

When I was growing up, the neighborhood began to change. More Colored families moved into the community. White families were moving out. They wanted to stay, but real-estate companies and builders told the Whites that the value of their property was going down because Colored people had moved in the neighborhood.

Many Whites wanted to stay in the community. They were hard working and just making it, but the real-estate people tricked them into moving. Then these same real-estate people turned around and sold the Whites' house to the colored people at higher prices.

I met more Colored children who moved into houses near mine. Most parents made the children "go outside." After a while, children got used to it. Playing outside became normal. We had to go and find something to do. So .... we made things and invented games!

One day, me and my new friends in the neighborhood saw a dead cat in the lot across the street from our house. Maybe the cat had been hit by a car. What Happened to the Cat?

That day, four of us Colored kids, two boys and two girls, were playing together in that lot. We were around 6 and 7 years old. We lived close to each other, either on the same street or just around the corner.

One girl was chubby, short, and brown. The other girl was skinny, short, and had real-brown skin. That was me.

The boys: One boy was chubby and had dark-brown skin. The other boy was light-skinned and was medium fat and sort of tough. The light-skinned boy was sort of a quiet bully. He made animals yell and run away if he got near them. He would even try to bop them with a stick if he could reach them.

We were all in the lot looking at the dead cat. The chunky girl said, "Let's have a funeral."

Everybody shouted. "Yeah, yeah, a cat funeral!"

"We need a box." someone said.

"I got a shoe box," I said, and I ran home to get an empty shoe box out of Mommy and Daddy's room. We were going to put the cat in it.

When I brought the shoe box back to the lot, we started fussing about who was going to put the dead cat in the box.

The chubby girl said, "I ain't doing it!"

"Me neither," said the chubby boy.

But that light-skinned boy, after giving us all a look, just walked over to the dead cat, picked up the tail with his hand, and threw the dead cat into the shoe box.

We were all shocked!!.

"Uggh ... Ugggh! … You're nasty," said the chunky girl.

That boy looked at us .... and just walked away. The rest of us looked at each other. *What to do?* we thought.

We looked back at that boy and began to follow him. Then we stopped. "We gotta have a preacher. Who's gonna be the preacher?" asked the chubby girl.

The big boy said, "That boy!"

"Yeah," we all agreed, "That Boy!"

"We need a hat; yeah, we need a preacher hat!" we shouted.

"My uncle got a hat!" said the fat boy. He lived down the block.

"I'll go get it," he said. He started running down the lot to go home and get the hat. His knees rubbed together when he ran.

"We have to put the shoe box in a hole" said the chubby girl.

We looked for a spot that had only a little bit of grass on it. We found a spot. We got some sticks and tried to dig a hole in the ground. The dirt was dry and hard.

We had been digging for a while when the fat boy came running back into the lot with his uncle's hat.

"I got it, I got it!" the fat boy said. He came running over to where we were. He threw a worn brim hat on top of where we were digging.

I snatched the hat off the ground and put the hat on "That Boy's" head, real hard.

He looked at me, expressionless, for a minute and then he pushed me out of his way. He kept on digging with the hat on his head.

We stop digging and stood up. "We gotta get in line," I said.

"You know, just like they do in church with the preacher talking real loud: 'GET IN LINE!'" I shouted.

"We gotta make a line behind that Boy—uh, I mean the preacher."

Then "That Boy" picked up the shoe box with the dead cat in it. He started making strange noises. "*OOOOOO ....ah hmmmm... oon ... huh, oom .. umm ....*"

We thought "That Boy" was supposed to be praying. "I never heard praying like that before," I whispered to the others.

"Me either," said the big girl.

The three of us marched down the lot, behind "That Boy.".

"We gotta sing a song," said the fat boy.

So the chunky girl started singing,

"Ole MacDonald Had a Farm, e i e i o.

And on his farm he had a cow, e i e i o..."

"A cow! This is a cat. We gotta sing about a cat," said the fat boy.

We started over.

"Ole MacDonald Had a Farm, e i e i o.
And on his farm he had a cat, e i e i o...
With a meow here and a meow there,
Here a meow, there a meow,
Everywhere a meow meow,
Ole MacDonal had a farm, e i e i o."

We marched around the lot and sang the song twice. Then we realized we needed to dig a bigger hole in the ground to put the shoe box in.

We only had sticks to dig with. So we all got our sticks and got in a circle around our little hole.

We were kneeling on the ground close together. After about 10 minutes, we all got hot and tired.

The hole we dug barely cleared away those tough weeds from the ground where we were kneeling. We had grass stains on the knees of our clothes.

"We gotta dig the hole deeper," insisted the fat boy. "That shoe box won't fit in this little hole."

Then "That Boy" grabbed hunks of grass with both his hands, threw the clumps, of grass behind his back and put the shoe box in the hole where the clumps of grass had been.

We all got real quiet. All you could hear were crows hollering and a dog barking from a neighbor's house down the block.

That Boy got up and went over to the grass clumps that he had thrown away. He grabbed big handfuls of that stuff and brought it back, putting it on top of the shoe box.

Then "That Boy" rubbed his hands together to get all the dirt and grass stains off. We just sat there. "That Boy" looked at us, stood up, threw the hat at me, and walked out of the lot. He was going home.

We all watched "That Boy." He walked home sticking and jabbing things with a stick.

It was getting hot, and we all wanted to go home. So we did.

When I got home, Ma made me a peanut-butter-and-jelly sandwich, on toast! I drank a glass of KoolAid with my sandwich. Then, I told Ma about the cat funeral. She said, "What!" I told her about, "That Boy" and what he did. Ma smiled. She said, "'That Boy' is your big sister's best friend's little brother. He likes to touch things."

The next day I went over to the lot. From her porch, the chunky girl saw me walking. She came running over.

The shoe box was gone.

"What happened to that cat?" she asked.

I shrugged and said, "I don't know." We looked at each other.

Then she asked, "You wanna play jump rope?"

"Yeah," I said. And we ran over to her house and got the jump rope. We jumped!!

"My Hero"

Ma packed the trunk of the car with a big box of food. She had put a loaf of bread, fried chicken, a homemade pound cake, and a big glass jar of cherry Kool-Aid in the box.

BEEP! BEEP! We heard a car horn. It was my Aunt Ellie, driving her car into our driveway.

"Will! I'm here!" Aunt Ellie yelled. (Ma's name was Willa; Aunt Ellie always called her "Will.")

*****

My Aunt Ellie was a six-foot tall, slender, dark-brown-skinned woman. She had real keen features, and her hair was just starting to turn gray. Aunt Ellie was younger than Ma, and louder too.

Aunt Ellie loved to walk barefoot ... even outdoors. She had some big long black feet, but she had no corns or bunions. Her feet were smooth. Only on occasion would she dress up—maybe for a funeral or a wedding.

Aunt Ellie loved jokes. Of all Ma's eight sisters, only Aunt Ellie loved to play tricks on her nieces and nephews. For example, sometimes Aunt Ellie would get real serious as if something important had happened. She would tell us a real serious story and look sad. Aunt Ellie would have our total attention. We would get serious too. Next thing you know, Aunt Ellie would burst out laughing at us. She would have a little glint in her eyes and a grin on her face. She would pretend to be innocent like she hardly knew what we caught her doing. She was a great actress. She would fool us every time.

Even our serious Daddy liked Aunt Ellie. Once, we saw Daddy shake his head and laugh a few times when Aunt Ellie did something real funny. Now, if serious Daddy laughed at something Aunt Ellie did, she really had to be funny!!!

We loved going to Aunt Ellie's house to visit. In later years (when we were in our teens), we would get mad at Ma or Daddy and run away… to Aunt Ellie's house. She'd entertain us.

Aunt Ellie would cook the best hamburgers with an egg in it. She always had fresh food all over the place. Clothes too. She would just step over stuff and tell us to do the same thing. We did.

When we went to see Aunt Ellie, her daughters (my cousins) Cheryl and Jessie and my uncle Neal would be at home. My cousins would sit around mostly bored with Aunt Ellie's jokes and tricks. I guess they were used to them.

But to Aunt Ellie's nieces and nephews, her jokes and pranks were refreshing and new. She never ever scolded us or made us feel sad. Even if we needed it. She just gave us that trickster's look. We loved her a lot because, to us, she was unpredictable and acted young like us.

Aunt Ellie and Ma liked each other a lot.

*****

Ma hurried to greet Aunt Ellie. Aunt Ellie got out the car and looked at Ma. Ma put her hand over her mouth and started giggling. I always wondered what was so funny and why they always laughed when they saw each other. It was like they had a secret code or somethin'. They gave each other a quick hug and laughed some more.

Ma said to Aunt Ellie, "I'm just about ready to go. You got everything you need?"

"Hell, if I don't, I ain't gettin' it now!" Aunt Ellie yelled. Ma looked at her and giggled. Then they both began laughing again!

*****

Aunt Ellie was known to use "bad" words, we were told. As children, we pretended we were busy and hadn't heard what she said. We knew better than to pay attention to those words because we would be in BIG trouble. Those were "curse" words. I knew, if me or my brothers and sister spoke like that, we would probably have to leave the United States. I could just imagine the look on my Daddy's face …*Not me!!*

Funny, Ma always spoke sort of proper and never used any of those words. Daddy NEVER used curse words. Ma told me once that, if children and people used those words, it made them look ugly.

"So, Ma, is Aunt Ellie ugly?" I asked.

"She is to me when she uses those curse words," Ma told me. "Aunt Ellie is a grown-up, so she says those words sometimes. Pay it no 'tention. You use the right words, hear?"

"Are you a grown-up too," I asked Ma.

"Yes," she said, "but I like different words than those curse words."

Nobody cursed in our house—ever!! But Aunt Ellie spoke like that most of the time! As children, we got used to it. I mean, Ma had other sisters (along with five brothers), but Aunt Ellie was probably our most favorite Aunt.

*****

That morning when my brother and I saw Aunt Ellie walk up the driveway, our faces lit up with excitement. Aunt Ellie would be driving "down home" with us. ("Down home" was the farm in North Carolina where my Grandpa and Grandma lived and where Ma and her sisters and brothers were born and raised.)

Ma shouted, "All right, children, get your pillows and blankets. It's time to go! Come on and get in the car."

My brother and I grabbed blankets and pillows to rest or fall asleep on during the trip. We found our spots in the car and nestled in for the long 13-14 hour ride from New York to a little town outside Charlotte, North Carolina. Aunt Ellie got in her two-tone white-and-yellow Pontiac car. And off we went, one car following the other.

After we rode for about two hours, it got real hot in the car. My brother and I took off our shoes. Our feet were a-stinkin', and every so often someone would fart.

Sometimes those farts were loud and stinky, but some—the little sneaky ones—were quiet and had a ferocious smell! *Pee-uuuuu!* .... It was those quiet farts that smelled like a rotten egg.

"Who farted?" Ma would ask.

My brother and I would shout, "It wasn't me!"—even though it had been one of us.

We even sniffed the smell of a garbage dump in the car. We were on New Jersey turnpike. *WHEW!*..... "It stinks out here!"

About 30 minutes after we had passed that garbage-dump smell, Ma pulled over to the side of the road. We had to air out the stinky car.

My brother and I started accusing each other of farting. "You know you did it," he said to me. And at that time, he was right. But I denied it. I wanted him to be the stinky one. I think Ma suspected that it was me, but she was more focused on trying to get back on the road.

Once Ma had to stop on the side of the road because I had to do number two. (Back then, like a lot of folks, we called pee-pee "number 1" and a bowel movement "number two.") Other times, we had to pee in a cup while we were riding.

That was easy for my brother because his body is different than mine, but, for me, pulling down my panties while hiding my private area and sitting on that used cup was nasty. I had to squat down on the car floor, hold the cup close to my body while that car was moving and let it out.....

I would ALWAYS miss that cup!!! When I would pee pee, the pee pee would come out sideways and leak down on my hands and between my fingers, then drip on my feet and sometimes get on the floor. I did get *some* of it in the cup, but it was still yucky.

"Ugh, ugh" I yelled.

"What you yelling about? It's your pee," said Ma.

"It's all over my hands, and some is on my feet," I said.

"Wipe your hands and feet off and sit down," said Ma. I did.

We rode for several hours. My brother and I got real restless. Ma had to stop to let us do number 1 and number 2 on the side of the road. Aunt Ellie kept on going. She didn't see us stop. Back then, we didn't have cell phones. So we couldn't call her. We were alone.

Ma stopped at a truck rest stop to sleep for a few hours. She needed rest after driving for six hours. It was hard for Ma to rest because my brother and I was wide awake and restless. Finally, two hours later Ma started driving again.

Ma drove for several more hours and then she turned off the highway onto a big street. There were some lights on that street, but it was still dark. Finally, Ma turned off the big street onto a winding road. It was *sooooo* dark on that road that everything looked almost black. There were lots of big dark fields and sounds of strange animals in the air. There was a strange smell in the air. It stunk out there.

Ma drove down that winding road as my brother and I listened to cows moooing. and crickets singing. "Ma, …. MA, where we goin'?" I asked nervously. "It's so dark out here and it stinks. I'm scared."

"We're goin' to Momma and Poppa's house. They live in the country. We'll be there in a few minutes," Ma said.

Those few minutes seemed like forever.

About 10 minutes later, Ma turned off the road into a house with a big driveway. The driveway was next to a big wooden house on one side, and a skinny little wooden house was 'way over to the right of the dark driveway.

The big house was dark too. It was still night time, about 3 a.m. in the morning.

There were three other cars in that big driveway. One of them was Aunt Ellie's. Ma pulled in next to Aunt Ellie's car, which was parked under a big tree.

As soon as we pulled in the driveway, and parked, three growling dogs came running out from under the house. Those mean dogs were barking like they were going to eat us up. HOW SCARY! A light came on in the house.

The squeaky front door opened. A little lady came out the door and stood on the wooden porch. More lights came on in the house. Everyone in that house got out of bed to see who had just drove up and to welcome us.

"Wilm!" called the little lady who was standing on the porch.

"Momma!" called Ma. They both laughed as Ma got out the car and walked up to the porch and hugged my Grandma.

The door opened again, and some young people came out of the house. They were my cousins. Most of them were barefooted. Their skin was dark brown because they worked in the fields. They were wild and strange to me. But my brother acted like he was used to everything.

Then, there was Aunt Ellie! She hollered at Ma, "What happened to y'all? I looked for you and you were gone."

"I had to stop, the chillin had to pee."

"Oh," said Aunt Ellie. She understood. Back then, not many public restrooms were available to Black people, especially in the South.

The little Grandma sat down in a chair on the porch. "Where's Poppa," Ma asked.

"Inside," said the Grandma. Grandpa had rheumatoid arthritis. He was bedridden now. So Ma went into the house to see him.

Me and My brother had gotten out the car. We were just standing there when Ma went on the porch to hug our Grandma. We were still standing there when Ma went in the house to see our Grandpa.

Then Grandma said, "Come here. Let me see you." I got scared, but Aunt Ellie was there, so my brother and I took timid steps toward my Grandma. I went first.

That Grandma gently pulled me close. She looked at my face and hair. Then she looked me up and down. "Um-hmmm," she mumbled. That Grandma knew that I had been a little sickly. Then she smiled at me. I wanted Mommy.

The tradition in the family was to acknowledge every child individually. Every child was looked at and touched, one by one. Every child was told how beautiful or good looking he/she was. A fuss was made over each child.

"Tee-hee" ..... a muffled laughing sound came out of two cars that were parked in the yard under the tree. I turned and looked. I saw the shadow of some heads in both cars. Who were they??

Well, back then, because there were separate places to stay for "Coloreds" and "Whites," Blacks didn't usually stay in hotels. Instead, family members slept in their cars and under trees in the yard. Some of my boy cousins slept in the cars or under trees so the visiting family could sleep in the bedrooms. It was late summer, and it was hot, so it wasn't too bad to sleep outdoors.

Day was beginning to dawn. The sky was getting lighter. It was almost 5 a.m. Everyone was still up.

All of a sudden, there was a thundering sound, and the ground shook. A flat wooden buggy, drawn by two BIG mules, bounded forward from the back of the house next to the barnyard. On the buggy, stood a barefoot skinny little Black boy–*another cousin!*

The boy had on raggedy coveralls and wore no shoes on his dirty feet. He shouted real loud, "Whooooa, WHOOOAAA!" like he was a big man, as he pulled hard on the reins. I was mesmerized!!

Oh! I thought… **"MY HERO!"** To me, he looked like a king…

The two BIG mules hitched up to that old buggy seemed to be snorting. The big white mule had a black patch covering one eye.

He was blind in one eye. The brown one was named Ole George, maybe? He was younger and very strong. Both those mules had real big heads and big mouths. They were smelly too.

Ma came out the house. She took us inside to see Grandpa. He was in bed in a dark bedroom. He looked old and sickly. But, he looked big in that bed. Ma told us to say hello or something. "This is you Grandpa."

I got behind Ma as I looked at him. I said, "Hi," real low. Then we got a chance to lie down and go to sleep.

Later that day, I saw "my hero" cousin. He was running after a chicken that was walking around in the yard. He caught one of the chickens. That chicken was squawking and flappin' its wings as he held it by its feet.

Then "my hero" cousin grabbed the chicken's neck and started wringing it.

I was shocked! "What are you doing," I shouted in horror.

He said, "This chicken is for breakfast. I have to clean it and get it ready."

"Breakfast!" I said. "I'm not eating that!"

He started laughing. Then the chicken's head popped off its body, and the chicken's body, without the head, skirted across the backyard.
"Ugh...*ugh!*" I screamed.

But my cousin just laughed and said, "You city young'ns don't know about life on the farm. I bet you ate chicken in the car when y'all was coming down here. That old chicken you had came from the store. Everything we eat down here is fresh, even our chicken. I bet ours tastes better than yours."

I just looked at him.

My hero cousin had put a big pot of water on the wood stove. The water was boiling. He ran across the yard and grabbed the bloody headless chicken. He brought the chicken in the house and dunked it into the boiling water by its feet for a few minutes.

How yucky, I thought.

When he pulled the chicken out of the hot water, the feathers were hot and gooey. "Watch this," he said. In a few minutes he had plucked all the feathers off that headless chicken. That chicken was sticky and sort of light-yellow looking.

Then my cousin said, "They do the same thing to the chicken in the city in a factory, but you don't see it. It takes a long time before you get your chicken. So you eat stale old chicken, But ours is fresh. We catch 'em, kill 'em, and cook them right away.

They taste real good. You see all those chickens out there in the yard? That's fresh chicken! I bet you ain't never seen a live chicken! You a city girl"

"I'm still not eating it," I said.

It may have been 7 or 8 in the morning when everyone was called to eat breakfast.

I thought we were eating dinner in the morning! There was so much food on the table. There were grits, biscuits, bacon, eggs, molasses, sausage, and that chicken with gravy.

There were two big tables, and everybody found a place to sit. They loved being together and eating the food.

Somebody fixed my plate. They put a piece of that chicken on my plate. I looked at it. I ate a biscuit, and that's all.

Singing the Lord's Prayer in Church

It was Sunday. My brother and I were dressed for church.

"You all go on ahead to Sunday school. I'll be there for the 11 o'clock service," Ma shouted to me and my brother.

We ran out the back door to the path that led to the lot on the next street. My brother was in front of me. We crossed the street and started running through the lot.

When I was running, I passed the unfinished house that a builder abandoned. That's where my BF (best friend), Gail, and I used to play in the dirt and sand. I paused.

"Come on, Joyce," my brother shouted. "You'd better keep up!"

I didn't want to. I wanted to play in the dirt and sand with Gail. But Gail was nowhere around.

My brother was getting real mad. He knew that, if he left me, he would be in big trouble. I knew that too. So I started walking again. As I caught up with my brother, we walked past my friend Gail's Grandpa's house.

Thinking about Gail made me slow down again, but my brother said, "Come on!" We crossed the street to a little path which led to the church. We had to go down the steps to the side door to get in. This was a basement church.

Sunday school had started. My brother and I rushed to find our classes. (We were in different classes.) Sunday school lasted about 30 minutes, and we *always* finished by singing "This Little Light of Mine." Then we would get ready for church service.

The church got real crowded fast. I was looking for my brother, and he was looking for Ma. "There's Ma," I heard my brother yell.

Ma came and got us. Then Ms Brown came over to Ma. She was a very pretty woman. She had a little gray in her hair, but she had a pretty face. She wore high-heel shoes and a jacket that had fur around the neck. She looked like a movie star. "Praise the Lord," she said to Ma. "Hello, children," she said to us.

We stood close to Ma and said "Hi."

My brother wanted to go home where Daddy was, and he kept pestering Ma to let him go home. She finally said "All right, but you go straight home."

Well, I wanted to go home too. "Can I go home too?" I asked Ma.

"Oh no," she said.

"But why can't I go home?" I asked. "*He's* going home."

And that lady, Ms Brown, poked her nose in and said, "Oh, no, baby, we want you to open the service for us this morning by singing the Lord's Prayer."

I didn't want to sing the Lord's Prayer in front of all these people. Ma looked at me. "Okay, she can," Ma said.

Nooooooo!...I was screaming inside. But when you went to church and were asked to do something, you did it!

Meanwhile, I looked for my brother. He had all his things and came over to tell Ma he was leaving. She said "Okay."

Then he looked at me and started making funny faces. He stuck his tongue out and grinned with his finger in his ears. I was real mad at him. Then he left.

I went upstairs to the church service with Ma and Ms Brown. I knew I would be here for hours.

Ms Brown told Ma that she was gonna take me to the side aisle where I could get up front easier. I looked at Ma, and she nodded. So, I went to the side aisle with Ms Brown.

At 11 o'clock, the service began. Somebody said the welcome address and then ... "We will now have a selection by one of our children.

Ms Brown sort of pushed me forward, saying, "Go on."

I went up to the front of the church. I stood to the side, and some other lady said, "Come over here, baby, in front of the pulpit."

I wanted Ma. I just stood there shaking all over. There were a lot of people sitting in those seats. Then I saw Ma. She looked at me and nodded.

I closed my eyes and started singing. I really picked a key that was a little too high to sing the Lord's Prayer. But there was nothing I could do about it now.

The church was real quiet at first. I was singing very soft and very low. After I sang the first line, I heard someone say "*Ummmm-hmm!* Sing, child. Sing child.

I opened my eyes and some people had their eyes closed and were rocking back and forth. I kept singing. I sang a little louder. Then I got to the high notes, which were too high for me to reach. I sang as close to the high notes as I could.

Do you know those people started yelling, "Hallelujah! Praise the lord!"

Finally, I was finished, and the people clapped and shouted, "Thank the Lord; thank the lord!"

When I got back to where Ma was sitting, she put her arm around me. I whispered to her, "Can I go home now?"

She said, "No, you're gonna stay here with me."

I sat there. I felt better now that the singing was over. When the service ended, a lot of people came over to Ma to encourage her to keep me singing.

After that, I sang the Lord's Prayer pretty regularly during the morning service. Each time I sang, the congregation would shout, "Praise the Lord," "Hallelujah," or "Thank the Lord," while rocking an clapping.

Singing in church in front of all those people helped me to develop confidence in myself. When I was singing in church, whenever I missed a note or was flat, I just got more encouragement from the people. After a while, I sort of got real good, and I liked it.

Singing in church by myself, made me feel real good about myself.

Everybody would hum, clap along, and say, "Sing, Baby; sing to GOD!!!"

And I did!! I sang as loud as I could. I DID!!!

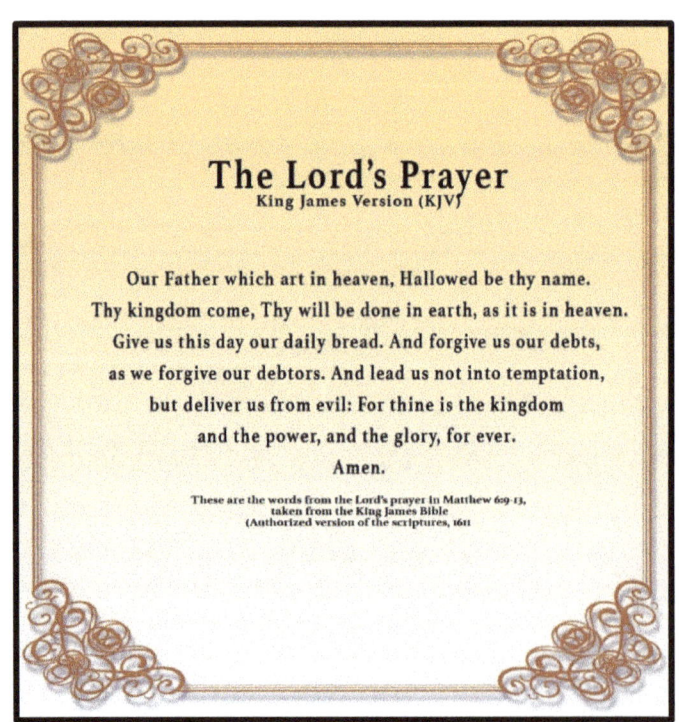

www.ingramcontent.com/pod-product-compliance
Lightning Source LLC
Chambersburg PA
CBHW041928040426
42444CB00018B/3466